WHAT'S SO FUNNY ABOUT PICKLEBALL?

A BOOK OF CARTOONS FOR PICKLEBALLERS by Jim Ditmars

Forward

What's so funny about Pickleball?

Pickleball players antics on court make me laugh, they just do- which is a good thing for a cartoonist! Some people want to win at all costs, whether in a tournament, or in Rec play, while others just want to have fun and get a little exercise. There's something for everyone. Young, old, knee braces, protective eyewear, false teeth…whatever. It takes all types from all walks of life.

Inside this book you will see players you recognize, and may even see yourself along the way.

Laugh at yourself, laugh with others. Have fun!

What's so funny about pickleball? Look inside to see for yourself.

About the Author

Jim Ditmars is an artist, retired public school art teacher (30 years), illustrator, caricaturist, and High School tennis coach with 25 dedicated years of coaching experience.

Jim's work has been published in the New York Times, the Beach Haven Times, the Sandpaper, San Diego Newsline, and on a CBS TV movie special entitled "Mystery at Fire Island". Jim collaborated with author Doug Snelson to illustrate a book of Pickleball Poetry.

While continuing to actively coach and play tennis, Jim was "STUNG" by the Pickleball Bug…literally- in the hand, the thumb, the head, the belly- OUCH! That plastic ball really does sting!

As Jim became an avid pickleballer, he noticed that a lot of funny things happen on the courts. He decided to illustrate these humorous happenings with pen, ink, and color as a way to chronicle this incredible game. The cartoons in this book reflect what many pickballers experience on an everyday basis, most of all while having a great time spent with others, growing, learning, interacting, and enjoying life!

Enjoy the book and enjoy the game!

**For my wife Mary Ann and my
children, JT and Patrick.**

They have put up with my pickleball "addiction"
for long hours and many a day and night. I am
extremely grateful for all of the support and
encouragement they have provided me
throughout my pickleball journey both as a player
and as an artist in search of the question…
"What's so Funny about Pickleball?"

PICKLEBALL
THE SERVE
Heh Heh... EASY GAME
I'M GONNA CRUSH THIS!
BELLY BUTTON
Rule 4.A.7.c
Contact of the ball must be below the Belly Button!
(Not above the Waist)
Duh!
DITMARS

THE
ATP
"Around the Post"
MY POINT!
IT DIDN'T
GO OVER
THE NET!
DITMARS

IF YOU ASK ME, HIS PREP IS GOOD, TECHNIQUE IS FINE, FEET NEVER TOUCH THE KITCHEN, BUT HE'S A LITTLE SHAKEY ON HIS LANDING!
SHEESH! EVERYONE'S A CRITIC.
START HERE
END HERE
THE ERNE
A HOP...SKIP...AND A JUMP!

THE TWEENER
WARNING
RESULTS MAY BE DETRIMENTAL TO YOUR HEALTH
OH MY ACHING BACK
BACK AT HOME
AHHH
FROZEN PEAS
T. MARS

SOMETIMES
LETTING GO
IS THE BEST SHOT

GREAT LOB MARGIE!
NOW WHO'S GOING TO CLIMB UP THERE TO GET IT?

BANGERS
UGH
BOOM
DINKERS
NICE and EASY
SOFT LANDING
CHEATERS
IT'S OUT! OUR CALL—OUR POINT!
Really?

PICKLEBALL
SIGN UP BOARD
WAYNE
ROB
MIKE JT
PATRICK
NANCY
ALEX JEFF
CHUCK
HANK
BILL RAY
TISH ANDI
DON
DAN DOC
MILLIE
RAVI
ANDREW
BOB BO
KATHY
SUPER.D
KATHY
I'll play with you if you are a
4.0 OR BETTER.
JUST STAY OUT OF MY WAY.
I have a
SUPER-DUPR!
THAT'S OK,
I'LL FIND
SOMEONE
ELSE.

NET INTIMIDATION

That's NOT the Date...it's the
SCORE!

WOULD YOU CONSIDER BEING MY PICKLEBALL PARTNER?
THANKS, BUT I ALREADY HAVE A PARTNER.
YES, BUT I'D BE MORE FUN TO PLAY WITH.
WHY DO YOU SAY THAT?
DOES HE POACH ALL THE TIME RIGHT IN FRONT OF YOU?
YES, HE'S ALWAYS HOGGING THE BALL.
DOES HE BLAME YOU FOR HIS MISSED SHOTS?
COME TO THINK OF IT...
I'LL SHARE THE ENTIRE COURT WITH YOU!
THAT SOUNDS INVITING!
I'LL EVEN OFFER ADVICE ONLY WHEN YOU ASK FOR IT.
THAT I COULD LIVE WITH.
WELL, WHAT DO YOU SAY TO MY PROPOSAL?
I ACCEPT! YOU'RE MY NEW PICKLEBALL PARTNER!
WHAT HAVE I DONE??? PICKLEBALL DIVORCES ARE NEVER EASY!

YES. I HIT LIKE A GIRL!
NEED A LESSON?
WHACK
LOOKOUT!

THEY DON'T CALL HIM
"NASTY NELSON"
FOR NOTHIN'!!!
WHACK
OOF
WHOMP

DON'T JUDGE
EASY
TARGET

OK. LET'S PLAY JUST ONE MORE GAME!
HE SAID THAT 5 GAMES AGO!

TOURNAMENT EVENTS

SORRY!
NOT SORRY...
TIC

REACH ACROSS THE NET FOR PEACE
PEACE
HEY PLASTI
HEY FUZZY
LITMARS
PLAYBALL

MY WIFE SAYS I PLAY TOO MUCH PICKLEBALL
MY KIDS SAY I PLAY TOO MUCH PICKLEBALL
MY PSYCHOLOGIST SAYS I PLAY TOO MUCH PICKLEBALL
EVEN MY GOOD FRIENDS SAY I PLAY TOO MUCH PICKLEBALL
BUT MY PICKLEBALL FRIENDS SAY I DON'T PLAY ENOUGH...
I GUESS BALANCE IS THE KEY. I'M JUST A LITTLE OFF BALANCE!
IN A PICKLE

IF YOU LIVE NEAR A LIGHTHOUSE,
YOU MIGHT HEAR THIS EXCUSE!

AHHH! THE LIGHTHOUSE LIGHT GOT IN MY EYES! LET'S HAVE A DO-OVER...

THEY SAID IF WE TRIED PICKLEBALL JUST ONCE, WE WOULD BE ADDICTED.
I DON'T SEE IT.
DON'T LET ANYONE TAKE THIS COURT!
DINKS WELL WITH OTHERS
HIS
HERS
PICKLE
H2O
MED KIT

WELL DOC, IT ALL STARTED WHEN I BEGAN PLAYING THIS GAME CALLED PICKLEBALL. BLAH, BLAH, BLAH...
THIS IS GOING TO BE A LONG SESSION. I BETTER CANCEL MY 8 O'CLOCK MEETUP
Psychiatry.
USPA MEMBER

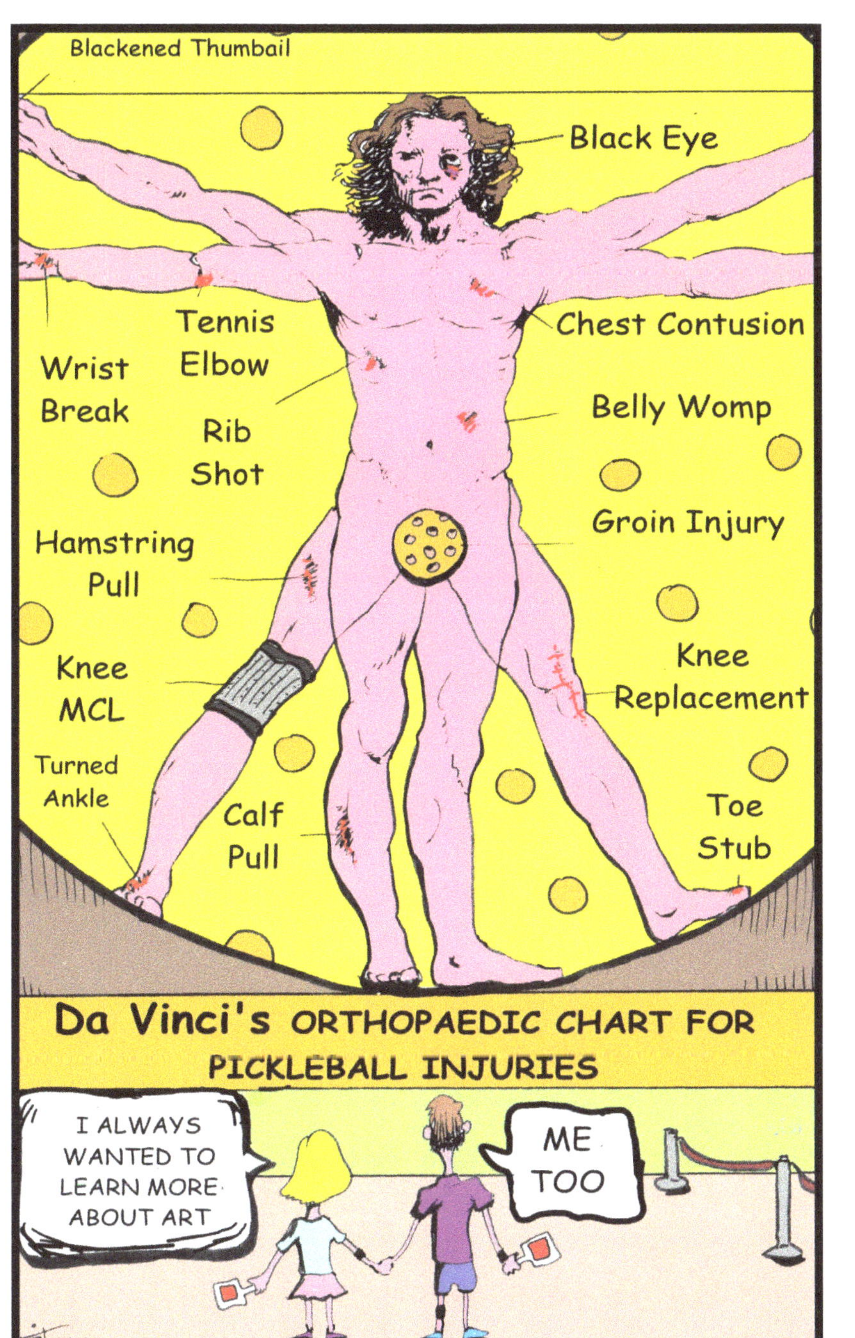

Blackened Thumbail
Black Eye
Wrist Break
Tennis Elbow
Rib Shot
Chest Contusion
Belly Womp
Hamstring Pull
Groin Injury
Knee MCL
Knee Replacement
Turned Ankle
Calf Pull
Toe Stub
Da Vinci's ORTHOPAEDIC CHART FOR PICKLEBALL INJURIES
I ALWAYS WANTED TO LEARN MORE ABOUT ART
ME TOO

ASK THE REF
Nice Job Ladies!
On The Next Point, Try
NOT To Hit At The REF
Please!

Time In.
0-0-2
WHACK

OK, SO WHAT'S THE
SCORE
AND WHO'S
SERVE
IS IT?
WHO STARTED
SERVING?
NO, WAIT!
THIS IS THE
FIRST POINT!
I THOUGHT
I
ALREADY
SERVED?

IN
OUT
???
SINCE NO INSTANT REPLAY CAMERAS WERE AVAILABLE, WE DEFERRED TO OUR
CRACK TEAM
OF
EXPERTS
TO HELP MAKE THE CALL...
DEFINITELY IN
NOT SURE... WHERE'S MY GLASSES?
OUT... MAYBE?
THAT'S OUT FOR SURE!
IS IT IN OR OUT?

OUT!
OUR POINT.

THE BALL HIT YOU! YOU SAID OUCH! OUR POINT.

SO, I GET
TWO POINTS FOR
HITTING EXTRA HARD,
DON'T I ?
ONLY IF
YOU'RE ON
MY TEAM

IF PADDLES COULD TALK!
WHY ARE YOU LOOKING AT ME LIKE THAT? IT'S YOU... NOT ME!
HOW RUDE!

Practice as he may, the **Paddle** always seemed to be the Problem

PICK YOUR PADDLE
SALE
SALE
PING PONG
PLYWOOD
XTRA LONG
OVAL
BASIC 16 MM
HYBRID STYLE
ERGONOMIC 14MM
BIG SWEET SPOT FOAM INJECTED PRO
CAN I GET A CUSTOM PADDLE MADE JUST FOR ME?
CERTAINLY. HOW WOULD YOU LIKE TO FINANCE THAT?
$
PRO
DITMARS

AFTER PLAYING FOR 3 STRAIGHT HOURS, RALPH DECIDED
IT MIGHT BE TIME FOR A WATER BREAK!

COURT OPEN !
OK, UP NEXT IS JOE, JOHN, and...
...uh...
ANYONE RECOGNIZE THIS HANDWRITING?
MARY ANN
JIM
PATRICK
VIC
SANDY
ANDY
KARL
GLENN
BILL
RON
JASON
JOE
JOHN

HAVE YOU PLAYED WITH JOYCE YET?
NO! SHE'S TOO GOOD FOR ME
WHAT IF SHE GAVE YOU A HANDICAP?
SHE OFFERED THAT.
AND?
I DON'T THINK IT WAS A FAIR OFFER.
WHY NOT? WHAT DID SHE OFFER?
DON'T ASK!
C'MON... WHAT WAS IT?
WELL...
WELL WHAT?
SHE OFFERED TO PLAY ME LEFT HANDED.
THAT SOUNDS FAIR. WHAT'S THE PROBLEM?
SHE'S LEFT HANDED!

HOW ABOUT A LESSON
I've Taught Her Everything I Know. Something Tells Me She Wasn't Paying Full Attention.
0-0-2 Where'd They Go?
THIS END UP
D.TMARS

YOU'RE DOING GREAT!
JUST ONE MORE HOUR AND YOU'LL BE PLAYING LIKE A PRO!
IT'S ONLY BEEN 5 MINUTES! UGH
WHOMP
DtMARS

WHEN HAND SIGNALS
GO WRONG!
STAY
?

THAT IS NOT WHAT IS MEANT by STACKING!
JUST A LITTLE HIGHER, HONEY. I'LL TAKE CARE OF THE LOBS. YOU GET THE REST.

JUST ONE MORE GAME
ARTIST'S DILEMMA
To Paint or to Play?
Bitmaps

THIS GAME HAS LEFT A LASTING IMPRESSION ON ME!
I'm IMPRESSIONABLE!
DITMARS

www.ingramcontent.com/pod-product-compliance
Lightning Source LLC
Chambersburg PA
CBHW040204160726
48006CB00014B/1887